10x-9/09-10/07
20x 5/14 ✓ 11/16

APR 2 7 2006

13x (11/00)
2/09

JULIUS CAESAR
and the Roman Republic

by Miriam Greenblatt

Marshall Cavendish
Benchmark
New York

ACKNOWLEDGMENT

With thanks to Michael Squire, Knox Fellow, Harvard University,
and Christopher Whitton, Kennedy Scholar, Harvard University,
for their invaluable help in reading the manuscript.

Marshall Cavendish Benchmark
99 White Plains Road
Tarrytown, New York 10591-9001
www.marshallcavendish.us

Text copyright © 2006 by Marshall Cavendish Corporation
Map copyright © 2006 by Marshall Cavendish Corporation
Map by Rodica Prato

Library of Congress Cataloging-in-Publication Data

Greenblatt, Miriam.
Julius Caesar and the Roman Republic / by Miriam Greenblatt.
p. cm. — (Rulers and their times)
Includes bibliographical references and index.
ISBN 0-7614-1836-9
1. Caesar, Julius—Juvenile literature. 2. Heads of state—Rome—Biography—Juvenile literature. 3. Generals—Rome—
Biography—Juvenile literature. 4. Rome—History—Republic, 265-30 B.C.—Juvenile literature. I. Title. II. Series.

DG261.G695 2005
937'.05'092--dc22
2004016678

Art Research: Rose Corbett Gordon, Mystic CT
Cover: The Art Archive/Museo della Civilta Romana, Rome/Dagli
Page 1: Museum fur Vor und Fruhgeschichte, Saarbrucken, Germany/Bridgeman Art Library; page 4: Bettmann/Corbis;
pages 6–7 & 23: Giraudon/Art Resource, NY; page 9: Alinari/Art Resource, NY; pages 11 & 14: Archivo Iconografico,
S.A./Corbis; page 15: The Art Archive/Museo Capitolino, Rome/Dagli Orti; page 18: Araldo de Luca/Corbis; page 26:
Ny Carlsberg Glyptotek, Copenhagen/Bridgeman Art Library; page 33: Sandro Vannini/Corbis; pages 36, 70, 80, 82,
85, 88: Scala/Art Resource, NY; page 40: Private Collection/Bridgeman Art Library; page 42–43: Leeds Museums and
Art Galleries (City Museum) UK/Bridgeman Art Library; page 45: Location Unknown/Ancient Art and Architecture
Collection Ltd./Bridgeman Art Library; page 47: Bildarchiv Preussischer Kulturbesitz/Art Resource, NY; page 49: The Art
Archive/Villa of the Mysteries, Pompeii/Dagli Orti; page 51: Museo della Civilta Romana, Rome/Giraudon/Bridgeman
Art Library; pages 53, 61: The Art Archive; page 56: Erich Lessing/Art Resource, NY; page 59: Private Collection/The
Stapleton Collection/Bridgeman Art Library; pages 63, 81: Museo Archeologico Nazionale, Naples/Bridgeman Art
Library; page 65: Réunion des Musées Nationaux/Art Resource, NY: page 68: Villa dei Misteri, Pompeii/Bridgeman Art
Library; page 72: Terme Museum, Rome/Bridgeman Art Library; page 75: The Art Archive/Musée du Louvre Paris/Dagli
Orti; page 76: Louvre, Paris/Index/Bridgeman Art Library; pages 78–79: Musée National du Bardo, Le Bardo,
Tunisia/Lauros/Giraudon/ Bridgeman Art Library

Printed in China
135642

Permission has been granted to use extended quotations from the following copyrighted works:
The Basic Works of Cicero, edited by Moses Hadas, 1951. Reprinted by permission of the Estate of Moses Hadas.
The Classical Roman Reader: New Encounters with Ancient Rome, edited by Kenneth J. Atchity. Compilation © 1997 by
     Kenneth J. Atchity. Reprinted by permission of Henry Holt & Co.
Inscriptiones Graecae ad Res Romanas Pertinentes. Rene Cagnat. Chicago: Ares, 1975.
"Caesar Invades Britain, 55 B.C." by Julius Caesar in *Eyewitness to History*, edited by John Carey, 1988.
The Law of Greco-Roman Egypt in the Light of the Papyri 332 B.C.–A.D. 640, 2e. Rafal Taubenschlag. Warsaw: Pa'nstwowe
     Wydawnictwo Naukoew, 1955.
"Buying a Farm, c. 170 B.C." and "The Mutilation of the Hermae, 415 B.C." in *They Saw It Happen in Classical Times: An
     Anthology of Eye-Witnesses' Accounts of Events in the Histories of Greece & Rome 1400 B.C.–A.D. 540*. Compiled by B. K.
     Workman, 1965. Reprinted with permission of Blackwell Publishing.
"191. Repeal of the Oppian Law, Rome, 195 B.C." in *Women's Life in Greece and Rome*. Mary R. Lefkowitz and Maureen B.
     Fant. London: Gerald Duckworth & Co., 1985.
"Founding of Rome" from *A History of Rome from Its Origins to A.D. 529 as Told by the Roman Historians*. Moses Hadas,
     Anchor, 1956. Courtesy of the Estate of Moses Hadas.
"Smiling Egnatius" from *Classics of Roman Literature: From the Literary Beginnings to the End of the Silver Age*. Harry E.
     Wedeck. 1963. Reprinted by permission of Reqeen R. Najar on behalf of the Philosophical Library, New York.

Contents

A Man of Contradictions

Julius Caesar was a man
of contradictions. He was
a military genius who
fought almost no battles until
he was in his late thirties. He
was bloodthirsty toward his enemies abroad but merciful toward his
enemies at home. He was Rome's chief
priest, yet he considered religious beliefs
to be mostly superstitions. A first-rate
politician, he courted the poor while
cutting secret deals with the rich. He
was an absolute ruler who rejected the
title of king.

**Julius Caesar was a great orator
as well as a first-class writer.**

In this book, you will read how Julius Caesar came to power more than two thousand years ago. You will learn about his various achievements, from conquering Gaul (present-day France, Belgium, and part of the Netherlands) to introducing the calendar we use today. You will read about the Roman family and the different religions that people of those days followed. You will learn about the kinds of work the Romans did, the foods they ate, the clothes they wore, and the entertainments they enjoyed. Finally, speeches, poems, histories, and legends will show you what the Romans themselves thought about their city, its political battles, and the Roman way of life.

PART ONE

Caesar strikes terror into the hearts of the Gauls in this nineteenth-century painting. The Gallic War lasted eight years.

The Master of Rome

Early Years

Gaius Julius Caesar was born on July 12, probably in the year 100 B.C.E.* His family boasted a very impressive ancestor. This was Aeneas, the legendary Trojan prince whose descendant Romulus was supposed to have founded Rome in 753 B.C.E. Since Aeneas was believed to be the son of the goddess Venus, Julius Caesar had one of the best pedigrees a Roman could have.

A good pedigree was important politically. Ever since the Romans had overthrown their last king and set up a republic in 509 B.C.E., Rome had been governed primarily by the Senate. Most of its members were patricians, or wealthy landowners from well-established families. Senators served for life. They wrote the republic's laws and handled its finances and foreign relations. Assemblies of all male citizens, which were strongly influenced by the Senate, played a lesser role in the government. One Assembly voted on whether or not to approve the laws the Senate had written. Another Assembly declared war and elected the higher-ranking government officials. The most important of these officials were the two consuls who were chosen each year. The consuls served as

*Many systems of dating have been used by different cultures throughout history. This series of books uses B.C.E. (Before Common Era) and C.E. (Common Era) instead of B.C. (Before Christ) and A.D. (Anno Domini) out of respect for the diversity of the world's peoples.

Julius Caesar began training for political leadership as a young boy.

chief executives and led the army in battle. At least one of the consuls was a patrician.

As the only son of a patrician family, Julius Caesar received a first-rate education. From his mother, he learned the traditional Roman virtues of honesty, dignity, discipline, and courage. From his tutor, he learned to write Latin in a clear yet forceful manner. He also learned Greek. Despite having a slight build, he trained hard and became an excellent swordsman. He was also a handsome youth, who liked to dress well and to wear his hair in a fancy style. It was a considerable blow to his pride when he became bald in his later years.

By the time Caesar reached his teens, the political situation in Rome was extremely unstable. Two main political groups had developed. One group was known as *populares,* because they appealed directly to ordinary people. Some *populares* were political reformers who felt the government had become corrupt and was ignoring the welfare of the average Roman. They wanted to take over the public land the rich had grabbed for themselves and distribute it to unemployed citizens. Other *populares* were military strongmen who wanted power for themselves. Also, they were convinced that the Senate was unable to govern the empire effectively. Opposed to the *populares* were the *optimates,* the "best men." They included most senators, as well as other people, mostly well-to-do, who wanted to keep things the way they were.

Although a patrician, Julius Caesar was connected to the *populares.* Their leader, Gaius Marius, was Caesar's uncle by marriage. When Caesar himself married (at the age of sixteen), he chose as his wife a young woman named Cornelia, who was the daughter of one of Marius's close associates.

In the meantime, another of Marius's associates, Lucius Cornelius Sulla, decided to switch sides and take over leadership of the *optimates.* The struggle between the *populares* and the *optimates* soon turned into civil war.

When Sulla left Rome to fight a war in Greece and Asia Minor

Marius's troops were nicknamed "Marius's mules" because they had to carry their supplies and gear in heavily forested or mountainous country where mules and carts could not go.

(present-day Turkey), Marius murdered many of Sulla's supporters and seized power. Marius died not long afterward. A few years later, at the war's end, Sulla returned to Rome and in turn murdered thousands of *populares*.

If Caesar had been older than nineteen, he probably would have been killed, too. Instead, Sulla demanded that he divorce Cornelia and marry a woman connected to the *optimates*. Caesar refused, and fled Rome for central Italy. Although he was allowed to return after a time, Sulla insisted on a face-to-face meeting. Afterward, he made a prophetic remark to members of Caesar's family who had urged him to be merciful. "Keep him since you so wish, but I would have you know that this young man who is precious to you will one day overthrow the aristocratic party, which you and I have fought so hard to defend. There are many Mariuses in him."

A Rising Star

Although Caesar was now a free man, his family thought it prudent for him to avoid any further attention from Sulla. Accordingly, a post for Caesar was found in Asia Minor. There he saw his first battle, the capture of a town called Mytilene. In the course of the attack, Caesar apparently saved a wounded fellow soldier at the risk of his own life. As a reward for his action, he received the oak wreath, or civic crown. That entitled him to sit in the front row at public games, next to members of the Senate.

Three years later, Sulla died, and Caesar returned to Rome. Anxious to begin making a name for himself politically, he decided to take advantage of the fact that he was a talented speaker. Two of Sulla's supporters stood accused of looting, pillaging, and extorting money from the public. Caesar prosecuted the lawsuits against both men. Although he lost the cases, his dramatic and forceful arguments in court gained him favorable attention.

Determining to become an even better public speaker, Caesar then set sail for the island of Rhodes to study with a famous Greek orator named Apollonius. On the way, the ship was captured by pirates, who demanded a ransom of twenty talents (between $100,000 and $200,000 in today's money) for Caesar. Imagine the pirates' surprise when Caesar burst out laughing. "Only twenty talents?" he exclaimed, and he offered to pay fifty (between $500,000 and $1 million)!

Caesar borrowed the money for his ransom and was freed after a captivity of thirty-eight days. He then assembled an army, attacked the pirate stronghold, and crucified his former captors. This incident gained him the reputation of being a dangerous man to cross.

In 73 B.C.E., Caesar again returned to Rome and immediately plunged into public life. His first act was to accept nomination to the College of Pontiffs, the group of priests that oversaw the religious life of Rome. Although the post had little political power, it had a lot of prestige.

Caesar's second step up the political ladder was more significant. He ran for quaestor, a position that involved supervising government finances. Running for quaestor was expensive, though, for many voters in the Assembly expected to be bribed for their support. Caesar had no money. But he did have a friend named Marcus Licinius Crassus, who was the richest man in Rome. Crassus loaned Caesar the money he needed, and Caesar won the election. He served for two years in southern Spain. Although he found the work boring, he was a careful and hardworking administrator.

When his term as quaestor ended, Caesar again returned to Rome. His wife Cornelia had died, so he took a second wife, Pompeia. She was a granddaughter of Sulla, the late leader of the *optimates*, which meant that Caesar was marrying into the enemy camp. More importantly, Pompeia's parents were rich. Between Crassus and his new wife's family, Caesar now had ample financial support for his political career.

In 65 B.C.E., Caesar held the office of aedile, a position that involved supervising trade, maintaining public streets and buildings,

Gladiators often fought against animals as well as against one another.

and providing large-scale entertainments for Rome's inhabitants.
Caesar put on the most spectacular public games the city had ever
seen, using his own money as well as government funds. There
were gladiatorial fights with hundreds of gladiators armored in
silver. There were chariot races and wild beast hunts. There were
stage plays, parades, and public banquets. The Romans loved it,
and Caesar's popularity grew by leaps and bounds.

The Catilinarian Conspiracy

The year 63 B.C.E. was a significant one for Caesar. He was elected *pontifex maximus,* or chief priest of Rome's state religion, a life-long position. He also won election for the post of praetor, or senior judge. After completing his term as praetor, he could look forward to being appointed governor of a province.

The year 63 B.C.E. was also significant because it marked a major public clash between Caesar and a politician named Marcus Tullius Cicero. Cicero was what the Romans called a "new man."

None of his ancestors had held high public office. Nevertheless, he had succeeded in being elected consul in 64 B.C.E., in part because he was a superb orator. In addition, he was supported by the *optimates,* who

Cicero was a prolific letter writer. He sometimes wrote three letters a day to the same person.

strongly disliked his opponent, Lucius Sergius Catilina, or Catiline. Catiline supposedly wanted to cancel people's debts and divide the nobles' estates among the poor.

Catiline ran for consul again in 63 B.C.E. and was again defeated. Stung by his two electoral defeats, he then organized a conspiracy to set Rome on fire and seize control of the government. News of his plans leaked out, however, and most of those involved were arrested. (Catiline managed to escape but was killed in fighting in central Italy.) When the Senate met to consider the fate of the conspirators, Cicero called for their execution.

Caesar objected. He pointed out that under the law, the conspirators, as Roman citizens, were entitled to a trial. Then, too, the traditional punishment for a senator who plotted a rebellion without carrying it out was exile, not death. Caesar suggested that an appropriate penalty for the conspirators would be life imprisonment in some secure town. Most important of all, Caesar said, there had been enough bloodshed over the past years. It was time for Rome's opposing political groups to work together.

In spite of Caesar's appeal, the Senate voted in favor of the death penalty, and Cicero promptly ordered the conspirators strangled. Public opinion at first ran strongly in Cicero's favor. He had saved the republic, everyone said. Then public opinion began to change. A number of officials condemned the executions, and more and more Romans decided that they were an abuse of power by the Senate. As the Senate's reputation went down, that of Caesar went up. People admired his political courage and moderation.

The First Triumvirate

Among the leading figures in Rome at this time was a man named Gnaeus Pompeius Magnus, or Pompey the Great. He had made a name for himself in 67 B.C.E. when he swept the Mediterranean Sea clean of pirates, thus enabling grain ships to move freely from Egypt to Rome. The following year, the Senate gave him the task of leading an army against Mithridates VI, a king in Asia Minor. Mithridates had already fought two wars against Rome. He lost the first war; the second was a draw. Now he was again trying to drive the Romans out of Asia.

Pompey defeated Mithridates and added several rich provinces to the Roman empire. In 62 B.C.E., he returned to Rome, expecting a hero's welcome from the Senate. He even disbanded his army before entering the city to show that, unlike Sulla, he had no intention of seizing power. Instead of expressing gratitude, however, the Senate rejected his request to give his veteran soldiers plots of land to farm. The Senate also refused to approve the territorial arrangements he had made in Asia. Pompey was furious.

Soon after, Caesar returned from the western part of Spain, where he had been provincial governor. The experience had been both interesting and lucrative. While subduing several hill tribes, he discovered that he was very good at warfare. He knew just how

One result of Rome's battle victories was an increase in the number of people
sold into slavery.

to place his soldiers and when to release his reserves for the final assault. He also made a tremendous amount of money by looting towns, selling prisoners of war as slaves, and taking a share of the local taxes. As a result, he was able to pay off all his debts.

It was the custom for victorious generals to receive a triumphal parade when they returned to Rome. However, Caesar wanted to run for consul. The Senate refused to change a law which stated that he could not do both. To Caesar, power was more important than "one day's glory." So he gave up the triumph and became a candidate for consul. He also began looking around for allies who might help him challenge the *optimates'* control of the government.

The Senate had hoped to squelch the ambitions of both Pompey and Caesar. But its treatment of the two men backfired. Instead of reinforcing its authority, the Senate's actions led to an alliance between Pompey and Caesar in which they agreed to support each other politically. To strengthen their relationship, Pompey later divorced his wife and married Caesar's daughter, Julia.

At Caesar's urging, the alliance was expanded to include Marcus Licinius Crassus. The resulting triumvirate, or "group of three men," was a masterful combination of resources. As one historian has pointed out, "Pompey had the army, Crassus had the money, and Caesar, a political genius, had the support of the people."

The First Triumvirate, as it has come to be known, was formed in 60 B.C.E. It soon began scoring one success after another. First, Caesar was elected consul. Then the Senate agreed after all to give plots of land to Pompey's veterans and to approve the territorial arrangements Pompey had made in Asia. Crassus obtained passage of a financial bill that would enable him to become richer than ever.

Although Caesar was only one of two consuls, his fellow consul,

Marcus Calpurnius Bibulus, was so ineffectual that people described the consulate as that of "Julius and Caesar" instead of "Bibulus and Caesar." All Bibulus did was declare most of the year a public holiday so that no laws could be passed. He then shut himself up in his house. Caesar simply ignored him and went on about his business.

Caesar tried to make the government fairer and more open. For example, he changed the administration of the provinces to reduce corruption by provincial governors. He persuaded the Senate to give land to many of Rome's poor. He set up a system under which the laws passed by the Senate and the Assembly were recorded every day so that citizens could read them and know what was going on.

Caesar also looked ahead. There was always the possibility the triumvirate might not stick together, especially since Pompey was as ambitious as Caesar. What Caesar needed was what Pompey already had: an army loyal to himself. Accordingly, Caesar persuaded the Assembly to put him in charge of three provinces after his term as consul was up. Not only that: his military command was to last for five years instead of the usual one-year term. It was later extended for an additional five years.

Military Challenges

In 58 B.C.E., Caesar set out to govern the provinces of Illyricum, Cisalpine Gaul, and Transalpine Gaul. Illyricum ran along the eastern coast of the Adriatic Sea. Cisalpine Gaul lay in northern Italy, and Transalpine Gaul covered southern France. The area north of Transalpine Gaul, Free Gaul, was as yet unconquered. It was inhabited by a number of different tribes. The Romans looked down on the Gaulish tribespeople as uncivilized barbarians. However, although they lacked cities, they were skilled farmers, weavers, metalworkers, and breeders of horses. They were also excellent warriors.

Caesar spent eight years fighting in Free Gaul. Each summer, when food could be taken from the land, he led his soldiers out to do battle. Most winters, he retired to Cisalpine Gaul, where he could keep an eye on what was happening in Rome. Caesar also spent the winter months writing a series of reports about his accomplishments of the previous year. Like politicians today, he realized the importance of good public relations!

Caesar's campaigns during the Gallic War stand out for their brutality as well as their effectiveness. For example, after subduing a coastal tribe called the Veneti, Caesar had its leaders killed and its surviving members sold into slavery. He punished many defeated Gaulish warriors by cutting off their right hands after they surrendered. When two Germanic tribes, the Usipetes and the Tencteri, crossed into Gaul, he imprisoned their envoys and attacked the tribespeople. Most of the Usipetes and Tencteri, including women and children, were either massacred or else drowned while trying to flee.

This attack, which happened when there was supposed to be a truce with the Usipetes and Tencteri, shocked even the Romans. One senator went so far as to demand that Caesar be turned over to the two tribes as a war criminal. Caesar, however, justified his actions by explaining that the tribes could not be trusted to keep a truce, for their warriors had already attacked Roman forces even while a treaty was being negotiated. Caesar then made an eighteen-day expedition into German territory, ravaging the countryside. He later sent an apologetic letter to the Senate in which he explained that he had used terror tactics only in order to discourage other Germanic tribes from moving into Gaul.

In 55 B.C.E., Caesar set out on what was probably his boldest, most adventurous campaign. He crossed what is now the English Channel and invaded Britain, many of whose inhabitants had been giving aid to the Gauls. To the Romans of that day, Britain was a mysterious island somewhere near the edge of the world. It had "strange, white cliffs" along its shore and was rumored to contain vast quantities of gold, pearls, silver, and tin. It was also home to a breed of fast-running hound that was popular in Rome for hunting and dog fighting.

Caesar's first invasion of Britain was a disaster. A heavy storm destroyed much of his fleet, while the Britons launched several successful guerrilla attacks against his troops.

After only eighteen days, Caesar decided to leave the island and try again the following year. His second invasion, in 54 B.C.E., went better. He won several battles and arranged some diplomatic alliances. Although he was unable to add Britain to the Roman Empire, his exploits greatly increased his popularity at home.

This was just as well, for Gaul was once again aflame. In spite of Caesar's terror tactics two years earlier, a number of revolts broke out. The largest, in 52 B.C.E., was led by a Gaulish chieftain named Vercingetorix, who united several tribes under his command. Vercingetorix at first adopted a "scorched earth" policy. He destroyed local crops and livestock so that the Romans would run short of food. He finally attacked Caesar directly but was beaten back and

In this scene imagined by a nineteenth-century artist, a defeated Vercingetorix throws down his weapons at Caesar's feet.

retreated to the fortified hill town of Alesia. Caesar besieged Alesia, hoping to starve the Gauls out. Then other Gaulish tribes surrounded the Romans and besieged *them.* After four days of ferocious fighting on two fronts, the Romans succeeded in defeating the Gauls. Vercingetorix laid down his arms, and the revolt collapsed.

Vercingetorix was taken back to Rome in chains and eventually executed. In the meantime, Caesar changed his policy toward the Gauls. Instead of terror, he decided to try conciliation. He gave Roman citizenship to Gaulish tribesmen who had stayed loyal instead of taking part in the rebellion. He signed a separate treaty with each tribe in which he guaranteed the tribe's name, boundaries, and laws. He required the Gauls to pay only a small tribute to Rome, and he allowed them to keep their religion.

Historians evaluate the Gallic War in two ways. On the one hand, it almost doubled the size of the Roman Empire and brought Roman culture—including good roads and the Roman system of law—to northwestern Europe. On the other hand, the cost was high: widespread devastation, as well as reportedly one million Germans and Gauls dead, and another million enslaved.

Caesar vs. Pompey

While Caesar was conquering Gaul, the First Triumvirate was falling apart. The first casualty was Crassus. He had grown increasingly jealous of his fellow triumvirs because of their military exploits. Accordingly, after being named governor of Syria in 54 B.C.E., he launched a campaign against the Parthians (in present-day Iran), hoping to win military glory for himself. Instead, in 53 B.C.E. his troops suffered the worst defeat inflicted on a Roman army in 150 years. About three out of four Roman soldiers were killed, while Crassus's head was cut off and thrown at the feet of the Parthian king.

Crassus had always acted as a mediator when Caesar and Pompey disagreed. They had been disagreeing more and more. Pompey disapproved strongly of Caesar's ruthless behavior in Gaul. As a result, he began moving closer to the *optimates*, who played on his vanity. In 54 B.C.E. Pompey's wife Julia, Caesar's daughter, died in childbirth. This weakened the bond between the two men.

After Crassus's death, matters went downhill fast. For some time, Rome had been experiencing vicious riots and gang warfare. The streets were no longer safe. So the Senate called on Pompey—who had remarried into the *optimates'* camp—to restore order in the city. In addition, his military command in Spain was extended for five years. Caesar's command in Gaul was not.

This created a problem for Caesar. A number of senators hoped to have him prosecuted for using bribery and force during his year as consul. That could not be done, however, as long as he held public office. Thus, the end of his military command in Gaul would clear the way for the trial.

The struggle went back and forth. Each side was frightened of the other. The *optimates* were convinced that unless Caesar was deprived of his army and put on trial, he would destroy the republic. Caesar was convinced that the *optimates* were after his life.

Nevertheless, Caesar did not want another civil war. So he

597
POMPEJUS MAGNUS
d. 48 f. Kr.

Like Caesar, Pompey came from a patrician family. He was a first-rate general and war hero but a poor politician.

offered to give up his military command if Pompey gave up *his* military command. Instead, in January 49 B.C.E., the Senate appointed new governors for Caesar's three provinces. It also gave Pompey absolute power and, in effect, declared Caesar an enemy of Rome.

When Caesar received news of the Senate's action, he was camped on the north side of a small river called the Rubicon. The river marked the boundary between Cisalpine Gaul and Italy proper. If Caesar crossed it with his army, he would be committing treason. He hesitated. Then, according to legend, he saw a figure sitting on the riverbank. Suddenly the figure seized an army trumpeter's instrument and blew the call to advance. It was an omen from the gods! "The die is cast!" Caesar exclaimed—and he led his troops across the river into Italy. Since then, people have used the expression "crossing the Rubicon" to mean taking an action that changes one's life and cannot be reversed.

The war between Caesar and Pompey for control of Rome lasted from 49 B.C.E. to 45 B.C.E. Although Pompey had more troops, many were soft and lazy from not having fought for a while. The rest were "raw recruits." Caesar's soldiers, in contrast, were battle-hardened veterans. They also were extremely devoted to their commander. They admired him for his courage, his energy, his fighting skill, and the fact that he marched, ate, and slept with them. He also paid them well, in both money and booty.

Still another factor that helped Caesar was his ability to move quickly and decisively. First he swept down through northern Italy, prompting Pompey and most senators to abandon Rome for Greece. Then he struck at Pompey's troops in Spain. Since he was now fighting Roman citizens rather than "barbarian" Gauls and

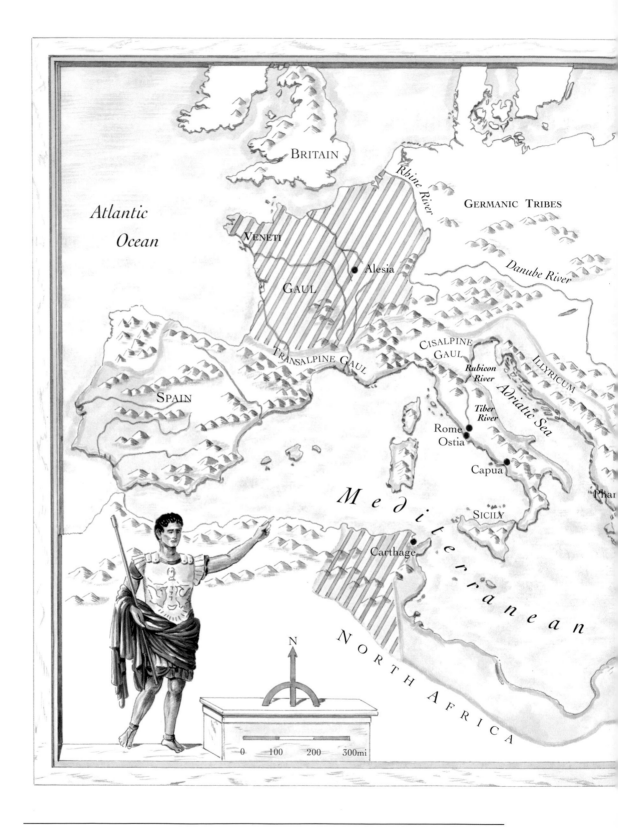

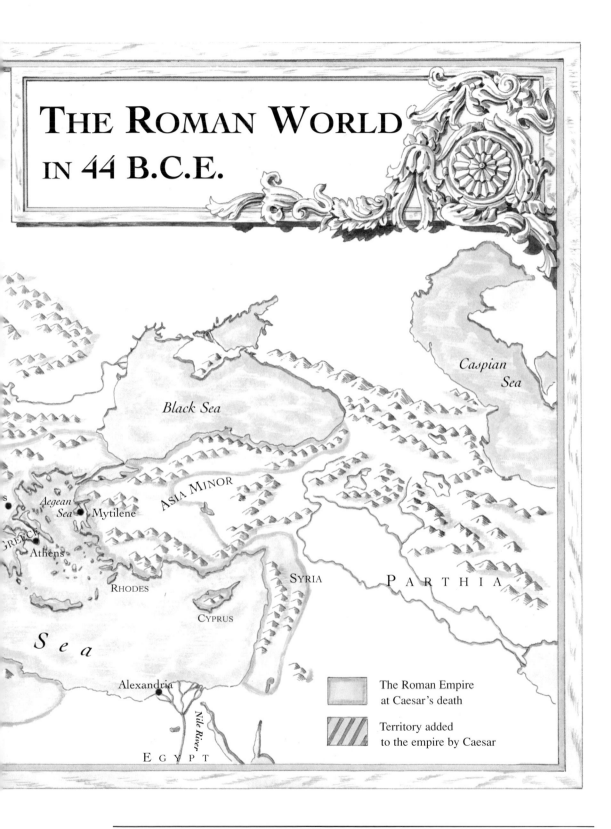

THE ROMAN WORLD IN 44 B.C.E.

Caspian Sea

Black Sea

Aegean Sea

Mytilene

ASIA MINOR

GREECE

Athens

RHODES

CYPRUS

SYRIA

PARTHIA

Sea

Alexandria

Nile River

EGYPT

The Roman Empire at Caesar's death

Territory added to the empire by Caesar

Germans, he behaved mercifully from the start. He tried to avoid bloodshed as much as possible. He pardoned his captives after each battle or siege, and welcomed enemy soldiers into his own army.

On his return to Rome, he instituted a number of governmental reforms. In just eleven days, he arranged for consular elections, restored civil rights to *populares* who had lost them under Sulla, and extended Roman citizenship to the inhabitants of Cisalpine Gaul, as well as to Spaniards who had supported him.

Most important of all, Caesar improved Rome's finances. For years, Romans had been falling deeper and deeper into debt. When the civil war broke out, financial activity stopped altogether. Rich people refused to lend any more money, while debtors refused to pay their debts. Caesar compromised. On the one hand, he forbade Romans from hoarding money. On the other hand, he allowed debtors to use land as well as cash to repay their loans. Since both lenders and borrowers got something, if not everything they wanted, money began to circulate again and a major crisis was averted.

Caesar had tried several times to make peace with Pompey, only to have his overtures either rejected or ignored. Now he moved directly against his enemy. He assembled a small fleet and in January 48 B.C.E., instead of waiting for spring weather, crossed the Adriatic Sea to Greece with about half his troops. The second half crossed over four months later.

After some preliminary skirmishes, the decisive battle between the two former triumvirs took place on August 9 on the plain of Pharsalus in east-central Greece. Pompey's army was more than twice the size of Caesar's. Caesar, however, was a far better tactician. He succeeded in setting two traps for Pompey's forces, pitting his infantry against his opponent's cavalry. By the end of the day,

15,000 of Pompey's men had been killed and another 24,000 had been captured. Caesar's losses numbered about 1,000.

Pompey then fled to Egypt and was murdered there in September. A few days later, Caesar likewise set foot on Egyptian soil—and encountered a new kind of adventure.

Caesar and Cleopatra

Egypt in those years was theoretically an independent kingdom ruled by a Greek dynasty that was descended from one of Alexander the Great's generals. In practice, Egypt usually did what Rome wanted it to do.

When Caesar arrived in Egypt, he found the country in the midst of a power struggle for the throne. On one side was the boy-king Ptolemy XIII. Opposing him was his sister Cleopatra VII. The pendulum had recently swung in favor of Ptolemy, who was then occupying the royal palace in Alexandria, Egypt's capital. Cleopatra was hiding in the nearby desert.

What Caesar wanted from Egypt was money. His troops had not been paid for some time. Deciding that the first thing to do was to heal the rift between Ptolemy and Cleopatra, he asked the two to appear before him. The men who had been advising Ptolemy agreed to the idea. They planned to intercept Cleopatra and kill her.

Matters turned out very differently. Realizing that her life was in danger, Cleopatra is said to have devised a scheme to bypass her brother's supporters. After entering Alexandria in a small boat, she had her attendant wrap her in a roll of bedding or carpet, sling her over his shoulder, and carry her into the royal palace to Caesar's

Cleopatra spoke seven languages, including Egyptian, Greek, and Latin.

apartment. "Once inside, she was unwrapped and introduced herself to the surprised but delighted" Roman leader. It was a daring act on Cleopatra's part—and it bore immediate results. The next day, Caesar called in Ptolemy and ordered him to share his throne with his sister.

It is easy to understand why Caesar and Cleopatra became lovers. He was fifty-two years old and the most powerful man in the western world. She was twenty-one years old, charming, graceful, and cultured, with a beautiful speaking voice. She was also very ambitious and a real gambler—just like Caesar. Caesar could help her attain—and hold—the Egyptian throne. Cleopatra, with her intelligence and her popularity among the Egyptian people, would make a far better ally of Rome than her younger brother.

After several months of fighting between the Romans and those Egyptians who supported Ptolemy, enough reinforcements arrived for Caesar to win what is known as the Alexandrian War. Ptolemy was killed in battle, and Cleopatra became queen of Egypt.

Caesar spent the next few months enjoying his first holiday in years. He explored Alexandria, with its white marble buildings, its public libraries, and its magnificent art. He took a cruise with Cleopatra up the Nile River in the royal barge, which was built of cedar and cypress wood and decorated with gold.

Accompanying barges contained musicians and other entertainers, while Roman soldiers marched in step along the riverbanks. In addition to being highly enjoyable, the cruise was an effective demonstration of Rome's power.

In June 47 B.C.E., Caesar left Egypt for Asia Minor, where the son of Mithridates, like his father before him, was trying to throw the Romans out. It took Caesar only five days to defeat his opponent. Writing to a friend in Rome, he described his victory in three words: *Veni, vidi, vici*—"I came, I saw, I conquered." In the meantime, Cleopatra gave birth to a son. He was named Ptolemy Caesar, popularly known as Caesarion, or "Little Caesar."

Ruler of Rome

The civil war should have ended with Pompey's death. But many *optimates* still saw Caesar as an enemy of the republic who had to be defeated. In their eyes, they were defending the long-established republican form of government against the evils of one-man rule. Accordingly, Caesar was forced to spend the next two years fighting the *optimates'* forces, first in North Africa and then in Spain.

In between these campaigns, in 46 B.C.E., he returned to Rome, where the Senate appointed him dictator for the next ten years. (In the past, dictators had been appointed only for six-month terms.)

The senators also gave Caesar what he had never received before: a triumphal parade. In fact, the senators gave him *four* triumphal parades, one each for his victories in Gaul, Egypt, Asia Minor, and North Africa. Caesar invited Cleopatra to Rome to see the Egyptian triumph. He also gave her the title of "Friend of the Roman People" and had a golden statue of her installed in the temple of Venus. He then established Cleopatra, together with Caesarion, in a villa on the banks of the Tiber River.

This last act shocked many Romans, for Caesar was still married to his third wife, Calpurnia. (He had divorced Pompeia.) Caesar, however, ignored the scandal. He had more important things to worry about. First he pardoned his enemies in the hope that this would bring about political peace. Then he turned his attention to Rome's economic and social problems. The city's population

A triumphal parade included statues of the gods as well as prisoners of war, soldiers, war booty, and a host of public officials.

had been increasing steadily in recent years, and many of its new inhabitants had no jobs. The potential for crime and violence was high, while the cost of giving the poor free grain added to Rome's financial burdens. Caesar decided that the best way to deal with the problem was to establish colonies for unemployed Romans throughout Italy and the provinces. More than 80,000 poor Romans soon emigrated to new homes. This not only reduced unemployment in Rome; it also helped spread Roman culture abroad.

In March 45 B.C.E., Caesar inflicted a final defeat on the *optimates'* forces in Spain. On his way home, he strengthened Rome's ties with its provinces by granting Roman citizenship to Spaniards, Gauls, and Greeks who had supported him.

Back in Rome, Caesar threw himself into the task of running the empire. He proved to be as bold and decisive in administering state affairs as he had been on the battlefield. He increased the Senate's size and filled it with his supporters, including both citizens from the provinces and wealthy Italian businessmen, such as bankers, merchants, and manufacturers. He lowered tariffs, reformed the tax collection system, and issued a new gold coinage. He punished rich racketeers and instituted more severe penalties for murder and other violent crimes. He began a vast public works program that included rebuilding Rome's harbor at Ostia and draining the Pontine Marshes near the city to prevent outbreaks of malaria and to create more land for farming. He tried to clean up traffic jams by banning all carts except builders' wagons during the daytime. He tried to cut down on excessive displays of luxury by limiting the number of slaves that could accompany the litters of rich men as they moved through the city's streets. He guaranteed freedom of worship to Rome's Jews.

He drew up plans for construction of a library grander than the main library in Alexandria, which was famous in the ancient world. And he reformed the calendar, replacing the old lunar, or moon-based, calendar with a solar calendar that had a leap year every fourth year. This solar calendar, which we use today, is still known as the Julian calendar in Caesar's honor.

The Ides of March

Caesar's activities greatly improved conditions in Rome. Still, many *optimates* resented and distrusted him. They disliked the fact that he had taken away the Senate's traditional powers. They were convinced he planned to abolish the republic and set himself up as a divine king. Didn't he wear purple robes—the color of royalty— in public? Didn't he sit in a gilded chair with a laurel wreath on his head? Just look at all the honors that had been heaped upon him! There were statues of him in temples throughout the empire. His image appeared on newly minted coins. His victories were to be celebrated annually. The month of his birth had been renamed Julius (July) in his honor. To top it all, in February 44 B.C.E., his term as dictator was extended from ten years to life.

This was too much for a group of some sixty senators. "Driven by a mixture of idealism, personal jealousy, ambition, and desire for revenge," writes one historian, they formed a conspiracy to murder Caesar. The conspiracy was led by Gaius Cassius Longinus and Marcus Junius Brutus. Both men had fought with Pompey and both, ironically, had been pardoned by Caesar. Moreover, Brutus's mother, Servilia, had been Caesar's mistress for many years, and some historians even believe Brutus was Caesar's son.

In March 44 B.C.E., Caesar announced the start of a military campaign against the Parthians to avenge their defeat of Crassus. Since he would be leaving Rome on the eighteenth of the month,

Caesar planned to address the Senate on the fifteenth, the Ides of March. When he awoke that morning, his wife Calpurnia told him about a bad dream she had had that predicted his death. A local soothsayer had made a similar prediction a few days earlier. Caesar ignored both warnings. He entered the Senate's meeting place— and was stabbed to death at the foot of a statue of Pompey.

The assassination did not save the Roman Republic. In reality, it had been dying since the days of Marius and Sulla. What remained was a shell that, many people thought, needed a strong leader.

Even Cicero, Caesar's old enemy, acknowledged, "We have killed the king, but the kingdom is still with us." After fourteen more years of civil strife, a strong leader did in fact assume power. He was Caesar's grandnephew and adopted son, Gaius Octavius, better known as Augustus, the first emperor of Rome.

As for Caesar, most historians credit him with spreading Roman culture throughout western Europe and around the Mediterranean Sea, and with laying the foundation for the imperial system of government under which emperors ruled the Roman world for five hundred years. They also credit him with devising battle strategies that are still studied in military colleges today. Even Caesar's name has been preserved in such titles for monarchs as the German "kaiser" and the Russian "czar."

Caesar's death has been commemorated in many paintings, plays, and motion pictures.

PART TWO

This mosaic of a wolf with two small figures was found in a Roman town in northern England. It is one of many depictions ancient Roman artists made of the legendary founding of Rome by the twin brothers Romulus and Remus. As infants, the twins were placed in a basket and thrown into the Tiber River, where they were expected to drown. Instead, they floated downstream and were washed ashore. A female wolf came upon them and nursed them. Later, they were raised by a shepherd and his wife. For more on the legend, see page 80.

Everyday Life in the Roman Republic

The Roman Family

The center of Roman society was the family. Its supreme authority was the paterfamilias, or head of the household. The household included the father, his wife, their children, and their slaves and hired workers. The paterfamilias remained the family head for his children even after they married and moved away. Only when a paterfamilias died did his sons finally become the heads of their own families. A man without a son to carry on the family name would adopt one from a family of the same social position as himself, or he might even free and then adopt a favorite slave.

In theory, the paterfamilias had absolute power over his family. He could divorce his wife if he felt like it. He could have his children banished or even put to death. In practice, though, he seldom made any important decisions without consulting all the family's adult males.

The only exception was in deciding whether or not to raise his newborn children. It was a Roman custom to leave sickly or deformed babies outdoors to die of cold or hunger. In addition, girl babies—who were less valued than boy babies—were sometimes exposed to the elements in the same way. Many, however, were rescued by childless couples or by people who raised them to sell as slaves.

Roman women could not vote or hold public office. They could, however, inherit property and pass it on to their children.

A woman's property was supposed to be managed by a male relative, but many women who owned property looked after it themselves.

Upper-class Roman marriages were arranged between families with an eye to increasing their wealth or improving their political position. Girls were married after the age of twelve, boys after the age of fourteen. However, a few men waited to marry until they were thirty or even older.

At the engagement ceremony, a couple signed a marriage contract and exchanged rings and gifts. A bride was expected to bring

A bride and groom join hands at their wedding. The figure between them represents Vesta, the goddess who watched over the hearth.

a dowry of either money or property to the marriage.

The wedding was held on a lucky day. Unlucky days included all of May and the first half of June, as well as certain days in each month. On the wedding day, the bride's mother dressed her in a long white robe and a bright red or orange veil, with a wreath of flowers in her hair. The groom, his family, and the wedding guests paraded from his house to the bride's house. There the groom took the bride's right hand in his, after which everyone said a prayer while a sheep or a pig was sacrificed to the gods. This was followed by an elaborate wedding feast, usually paid for by the groom. All the guests then accompanied the couple to the groom's house, where the new husband carried his wife across the threshold.

Most Romans married only once. Upper-class Romans, however, often divorced and remarried several times, usually because of the need to make new political alliances.

Growing Up

Nine days after a boy was born, his father named him and placed a charm around his neck. If the parents were rich, the charm was made of gold. If they were poor, it was made of leather. The charm was supposed to protect the boy from envy and harm, and he wore it until he became a man at the age of about sixteen.

A boy often learned to read and write from his father. At the age of seven, he started school, unless his parents could afford a private

Romans played knuckle-bones—a game similar to dice—with pieces of pottery or bone. The pieces had four flat sides and were rounded at each end. Each flat side had a number on it.

tutor. Education was voluntary, however, and was supported by fees rather than taxes. As a result, poor boys and farmers' sons usually grew up illiterate.

There were no school buildings. Each teacher held his own classes, usually in a rented room in a ground-floor shop. The teacher sat in a high-backed, armless chair. His pupils sat on benches. If a pupil misbehaved, the teacher would hit him on the hand with a cane or flog him with a leather whip. The school day was six hours long, with a recess for lunch. The school year was rather short, for there were many holidays, as well as a summer vacation.

Pupils studied reading, writing, and arithmetic. They wrote on a waxed wooden tablet with a pointed iron instrument called a stylus. They used an abacus to help them add, subtract, multiply, and divide. The abacus consisted of several rods on which were strung beads that slid back and forth. Learning arithmetic was cumbersome because the Romans did not use special symbols for numbers. Instead, they used combinations of seven letters: I (1), V (5), X (10), L (50), C (100), D (500), and M (1,000). Thus, where we write 84, the Romans wrote LXXXIV.

At about the age of twelve, an upper-class boy began the study of literature and Greek. (Lower-class boys would be working or learning a trade.) Learning Greek was important for two reasons. First, many great poems—such as the *Iliad* and the *Odyssey*—were written in Greek. Second, Greek was the common language for business and trade in much of the region around the Mediterranean Sea, including Egypt, Sicily, and of course Greece.

At about the age of sixteen, a boy became a man and a citizen of Rome. Accompanied by his father and family friends, he went to the city's political center, the Forum. There he put on a man's clothing and received a man's haircut and his first shave. If he belonged to a senatorial family, his education now included philosophy, composition, and especially oratory, or public speaking. All three were considered necessary for a career in government. Many rich young men then went abroad for still more education, the most popular destination being Athens, Greece.

A Roman girl received her name and her good-luck charm eight days after she was born. She learned how to read and write either at home or, more rarely, in school. Her mother usually taught her how to spin and weave. Wealthy girls often learned to paint, sing, dance, and play a musical instrument.

This boy is reading a scroll made of papyrus, a plant that grows along the Nile River in Egypt.

Occupations, Professions, and Trades

Upper-class Romans did not have to work for a living. Their large estates provided them with ample incomes. However, they were expected to devote themselves to public service. In practice, this meant becoming a lawyer, "a good man skilled in speaking." Being a lawyer was also the best way to enter politics. Since trials were held in public, a good lawyer soon became widely known. That made it easy for him to get votes when he ran for office.

A lawyer learned legal procedure not by going to school, but by being sponsored by an older lawyer. That involved attending the older lawyer's trials and asking him questions over the dinner table. A lawyer did not demand a fee for his services, but it was considered acceptable to give him a present or leave him a legacy.

In later years, lawyers split into two groups. One group consisted of consultants, who gave advice about the law in exchange for a fee. The second group consisted of advocates, who tried cases in court.

Ordinary Romans worked at a variety of professions and trades. Some were publishers and booksellers. The books were handwritten on sheets of papyrus, a form of paper, that were glued together and then wound over wooden rollers. A roll might be more than

Shopkeepers display their wares in this stone relief of a Roman cutlery store.

a hundred feet long. Scribes used a reed pen and a thick ink made of soot and resinous gums. The Romans wrote only with capital letters. Sentences ran into each other, since the Romans did not use periods.

Old-fashioned Roman doctors relied on such things as incantations or magical spells, magic well water, and potions containing human fat or blood. Gradually, however, Greek doctors and the study of Greek medical knowledge became popular. By Caesar's time, doctors were removing tonsils, performing eye operations, repairing hernias, and making false limbs of wood and bronze. Bloodletting was popular, and doctors commonly used herbs and herbal preparations. Unfortunately, ancient Rome lacked proper sanitation, to say nothing of vaccines and antibiotics. As a result, diseases such as malaria, typhus, smallpox, and tuberculosis were rampant. So were stomach upsets caused by spoiled food.

Banking was an important occupation in ancient Rome, which thrived on trade. Bankers worked at special tables set up in public areas. They changed money. They paid interest on deposits. They made loans to individuals. And they bought and sold land and buildings. The most common coins were the silver *sestertius* and the silver *denarius,* which was worth four *sestertii.* There were copper and gold coins as well.

Roman merchants imported goods from many faraway places. Egypt, North Africa, and Sicily supplied wheat and olive oil. Wine and copper utensils came mostly from Spain and Gaul. Britain produced tin, lead, silver, and oysters. India provided spices, and China furnished silk.

Some goods, such as silk, were carried overland, usually by camels and donkeys. Other products—such as grain, wine, and olive oil—

Romans frequently ate out in "fast food" shops like this one.

were moved by sea. The wine and olive oil were transported in pottery jars called amphorae. The size and shape of an amphora generally showed where it had been made and what it contained.

Cargo ships usually anchored in the harbor of Ostia, at the mouth of the Tiber River about fifteen miles from Rome. The goods were transferred to barges for the trip upriver, then, in Rome, were unloaded and stored in huge warehouses before being sold or distributed.

Most merchant ships sailed only during the summer. Owners preferred to keep their ships in port during the winter to protect them from storms.

Roman shopkeepers usually gathered together in one place to sell their wares. Originally, most shops had been located in the Forum. By Caesar's time, however, several additional commercial centers had developed. The Forum Boarium specialized in the sale of cattle and livestock. Romans looking for oil, fruit, and vegetables went to the Forum Holitorium. The shops that remained in the original Forum handled mostly items made of silver and gold.

Other goods—such as clothing, kitchen utensils, and books— were manufactured and sold in shops along the city's main streets. Streets were often known for a particular trade, such as the street of the cobblers or the street of the cabinetmakers. A typical shop had an open front, with a counter on the street. Some shopkeepers created a traffic hazard by displaying their wares on the pavement. A sign on the outside of a shop bore either a name or a symbol of the trade, such as five hams for a butcher shop. Most shopping was done by men and slaves, who always bargained over the price of an item.

Because many Romans lacked proper kitchens, they either ate

out or ordered food to go. The city contained numerous bakeries, "fast food" shops, and taverns. The taverns sometimes provided lodgings on an upper floor or gambling in a back room.

The fast food shops were frequently run by women. Women also worked as waitresses, bakers, weavers, shoemakers, fishmongers, and laundresses. Many were midwives, and a few were doctors.

The Roman Soldier

During the early years of the Roman Republic, every male citizen who owned property served in the army. At first these citizens served without pay, joining up whenever danger threatened. After a while, the government began to pay soldiers. It also began to

Roman legions were made up of from four to six thousand men. Every legion had a horn blower to send messages.

recruit them from people without property as well as from property owners. Gradually the army became a full-time profession.

Romans usually joined the army at the age of eighteen. A recruit had to be at least five feet eight inches tall, with good eyesight and hearing and all his fingers and toes. He also had to carry a letter of recommendation from a respected citizen. Men known to be dishonest or lazy were not accepted.

By Caesar's time, the average enlistment period was six years of continuous service, plus an additional ten years of off-duty service. Off-duty service meant that a man could be recalled to the army in the event of an emergency.

A Roman soldier's pay was expected to cover the cost of his weapons, armor, food, and bedding. In addition, part of his pay was deposited in a military bank as a form of compulsory savings. As a result, most Roman soldiers were always short of cash. However, a soldier was allowed to keep whatever booty he obtained in wartime. In addition, upon being discharged, he received either a cash bonus or a plot of land to farm. That made the army a popular career choice, especially for men of the lower classes.

Roman soldiers were organized into legions of four to six thousand men. By Caesar's time each legion had a number and a name. It also had a sacred image known as a standard, which consisted of a silver eagle mounted on a pole. The eagle was inscribed with the letters *SPQR*, for *Senatus Populusque Romanus*—"the Senate and people of Rome." It was considered a permanent disgrace for a legion to lose its standard in battle.

A legionary's armor consisted of a bronze helmet, lower-leg protectors, and either a leather breastplate covered with iron or a coat of mail on top of a tunic. The tunic was dark red so that it would not show blood. On his feet, the legionary wore leather sandals studded with nails. A thick wool cloak protected him against the cold. If the weather turned freezing, he sometimes imitated the Gauls and the Germanic tribes of northern Europe and put on a pair of "barbarian" trousers.

Roman soldiers were probably the best trained in the world. They were expected to march between eighteen and thirty miles in five hours while wearing full armor and carrying an average of sixty pounds of gear and supplies. They spent long hours practicing the use of their weapons—throwing javelins, thrusting with swords, and protecting themselves with wooden shields covered in leather and rimmed with bronze or iron. They also learned various battle formations.

While on the march, Roman soldiers built a fortified camp each night in which to sleep. The next morning, they burned the camp to prevent its use by the enemy. Laying out a camp followed a set procedure. First the legion's commanders chose a site and had it leveled if the ground was uneven. Then surveyors marked out where the streets and tents were to go. The officers' quarters, a paymaster's office, a marketplace, a hospital for the troops, and a hospital for the horses were placed in the camp's center. Each tent, which was made of leather, held eight legionaries, and the tents were always pitched in the same order so that the men could easily find their places in the dark.

The typical camp measured about two miles around. Surrounding it was a stockade, or wall, made of forty to fifty thousand wooden stakes. Outside the stockade was a ditch some three to ten feet deep. Between the stockade and the tents was an empty space about two hundred feet wide. The space enabled the legionaries to march in and out of their tents in an orderly manner. It also provided a storage area for cattle and other booty captured from the enemy. And it kept the tents out of range of enemy arrows in the event of a night attack.

Discipline in the Roman army was as intense as training. Good behavior was rewarded with either a gold or silver medallion or other decoration and perhaps a promotion in rank. A promotion meant more pay as well as greater authority and prestige. Punishment depended on the soldier's offense. If he showed cowardice

A Roman army camp resembled a small city, with administrative offices, a marketplace, and a section for craftsmen.

in battle, stole from the camp stores, lied under oath, or fell asleep on duty, he was beaten to death. If he committed a minor offense, he might be served inferior food or have to stand at attention all day. Sometimes he was transferred to the lowly navy.

The Romans told many stories about legionaries' brave deeds. One hero was Scaeva. While guarding the gate of a fortress, he lost one eye and suffered severe wounds in his thigh and shoulder. Nevertheless, he continued to fight. Another hero was Acilius. While he was trying to board an enemy ship during a naval battle, his right hand was cut off. But that did not stop him. He succeeded in boarding the ship and forced the enemy to retreat by shoving them with a shield held in his left hand.

Legionaries often performed civil as well as military duties, especially in the provinces. They built bridges and roads, patrolled streets and harbor areas, and carried official mail.

The Life of a Slave

Until about the second century B.C.E., most of the slaves in Rome were Italians. Only rich Romans owned more than one or two. Then Rome began expanding around the Mediterranean, and hordes of war captives began to pour into the city. (Unlike slavery in the United States, slavery in Rome had nothing to do with the color of a person's skin.) By Caesar's time, at least one quarter of Rome's population were slaves. Although poor people did not

These slaves use large rods, as well as their feet, to press grapes into wine.

own any slaves, prosperous families had from three to a dozen, while very rich families might own several hundred.

Slaves did all kinds of work. They were bakers and cooks, valets and ladies' maids, doormen and gardeners. Slave nurses raised the family's children, and slave tutors educated them. When a rich lady went shopping or visiting, she rode in a litter carried by six to eight slaves. A wealthy man was always surrounded by a bodyguard of slaves when he ventured outdoors at night.

Many slaves worked for Rome rather than for a family, building and maintaining public structures such as bridges, roads, and aqueducts. If they were unlucky, they were forced to work in mines, where they lasted perhaps one to two years before dying from exhaustion.

Many Romans treated their slaves decently. If a slave was a skilled craftsman or knew how to keep accounts, his master might hire him out or set him up in his own business. He could keep part of his fees, save his money, and eventually buy his freedom. Some Romans freed their slaves as a reward for years of faithful service.

Other Romans, however, treated their slaves brutally, and many ran away from their masters. In 73 B.C.E., a slave revolt led by a gladiator named Spartacus broke out. For two years, some 90,000 slaves terrorized the Italian countryside. Then they were defeated in battle and 6,000 were crucified along the 130-mile road from Capua to Rome. After that, there were no more slave revolts.

Food and Feasts

The staple of the Roman diet was wheat. The Romans either boiled it into a kind of porridge or baked it into bread. For variety in their diet, they added herbs, vegetables, and—whenever possible—salted fish and poultry. The Romans—except for the rich—ate meat only on special occasions, such as a marriage or a birthday.

The Romans seldom ate breakfast. If they did, it usually consisted simply of bread spread with honey or dipped in wine. Lunch

Eggs formed an important part of the Roman diet.

usually meant cold leftovers from the night before. The main meal, dinner, was served at about four o'clock in the afternoon, after the day's work was finished. It consisted of three courses. The appetizer was usually a boiled egg with olives and sardines, served on a bed of lettuce. The main course was porridge, sometimes flavored with a ham bone. Dessert might include apples, nuts, and honey cakes.

Rich Romans liked giving dinner parties with elaborate and often exotic menus. Appetizers at these affairs included such rarities as jellyfish and eggs or boiled tree fungi with peppered fish sauce. For the main course, a host might serve a boiled ostrich with sweet sauce, dormice stuffed with pork and pine nuts, sea oysters, roasted deer, wild boar, or ham boiled with figs and bay leaves. Desserts consisted of honey-sweetened cakes and fruits. Everyone drank wine mixed with water.

The average dinner party included the host and eight guests. Three couches were placed around a table, with three people on each couch. They stretched out, leaning on their left elbows, and ate either with spoons or with their fingers. Guests often brought their own napkins, which they used to carry leftovers home. Slaves usually stood by working fans made of bird feathers to keep flies off the food.

Dinner parties often provided entertainment as well as food. There were jugglers, acrobats, and clowns. Flutists and lyre players performed either by themselves or as an accompaniment to singers. Scantily clothed dancing girls sometimes added to the fun. On a more intellectual level, a slave might read the work of a Greek author, or a host might recite his own poems.

Clothing

Roman clothing was made mostly of wool. Both men and women dressed in a belted tunic, either sleeveless or with short sleeves. A man's tunic ended at the knees. A woman's tunic fell to her ankles. The color was usually white. Poor people's clothing, though, soon turned gray or brown since they could not afford to have it cleaned.

For political affairs, dinner parties, and other formal occasions, a man wore a toga over his tunic. A toga was basically a large piece of woolen cloth measuring about six feet by eighteen feet. It was wrapped around the body in such a way as to leave only the right hand free. The ordinary citizen's toga was plain white, but the togas of senators and priests were bordered with a purple stripe. A woman covered her tunic with a *palla,* or mantle. She pulled the palla up over her head when she went outside.

Roman women could drape their *pallas* in several different ways.

In bad weather, the Romans wore waterproof cloaks made from wool that had not been cleaned or bleached and thus retained its natural oils. Both men and women wore sandals at home. If they were going out, they put on shoes that laced up the front.

Making a garment took a long time. Women and girls spun raw wool into thread and wove the thread into cloth. The cloth was then sent to a fuller, who washed it and treaded it with his feet. That helped thicken it. Next the cloth was bleached with sulfur, washed again, and brushed with a comb that raised up a nap. After the nap was cut off, the cloth was sprinkled with water and pressed. All this work made clothing quite valuable. As one historian observed, "A toga only three or four times washed . . . [was] a considerable gift."

♥

Improving One's Looks

In early times, Roman men wore beards and long hair. From the third century B.C.E., however, they were clean-shaven and cropped their hair short. Fashionable city dwellers often perfumed their hair, while older men dyed it when it began to turn gray. A few older men put on wigs when they started balding. Others tried to stop their hair loss by rubbing their scalps with bear fat, marrow from deer bones, or a mixture of rats' heads and pepper.

Poor Roman women did not fuss much with their hair. Rich women, on the other hand, were always changing hairstyles. They curled their hair with curling irons, wore braids and bangs, and added hairpieces for body. Many dyed their hair blond.

Wealthy Roman women used a great deal of makeup. They smeared their faces with white lead or chalk; applied red ocher to their lips and cheeks; and blackened their eyebrows with ashes or a paste made from crushed ants' eggs.

Both men and women made daily use of Rome's public baths. These were magnificently decorated buildings, complete with a steam room and hot and cold running water. Many contained a library, a garden, and shops, as well as rooms for bathing, exercising, and getting a massage. The admission price was low. Furthermore,

Rich women spent many hours having their hair done.

a wealthy person—especially if he was running for public office— would sometimes pay everyone's fees for anything from a day to a year.

Insulae and Houses

Most city-dwelling Romans lived in *insulae*, or "islands." These were tenements built mostly of wood. They were usually five or six stories high, with shops on the ground floor and one- or two-room apartments on each of the upper floors. The typical *insula* covered a city block.

Life in an *insula* was uncomfortable and somewhat dangerous. The rooms were dark, since they had few, if any, windows. (Each floor landing, however, did contain two windows screened with wooden shutters.) There was no running water, so tenants had to fill their water jugs at a street fountain and carry them upstairs. There were no latrines, either, so tenants used chamber pots, which they often emptied into the street.

The danger arose from the fact that *insulae* were shoddily built and lacked a metal framework. As a result, they frequently collapsed, injuring or killing dozens of residents. Fires were another hazard. These were caused by the oil lamps that furnished light or by the charcoal-burning braziers that provided heat in winter.

Rich Romans, in contrast, usually lived in a large private house known as a *domus*. A *domus* contained two main parts, the public rooms and the private rooms.

The public rooms included an atrium and a *tablinum*. The atrium was a combination living room and reception hall, where the house's owner received visitors. It was partly open to the sky and

This model of a street scene shows an *insula* to the right and a *domus* on the left.

often housed the shrine to the family gods. The *tablinum* served as an office and library and also contained cupboards with wax masks of the owner's ancestors. The more famous ancestors a man had, the more cupboards stood in his *tablinum.* Both the atrium and the *tablinum* were often decorated with mosaics on the floor and painted murals on the walls. The furnishings might include gold and silver candelabras and tables of rare wood inlaid with ivory.

The private rooms consisted of bedrooms, baths, a dining room, and a kitchen. They were built around a peristyle, or courtyard. The peristyle was edged with marble columns and planted with flowers, fruit trees, and evergreen shrubs. Private rooms were simply furnished. A bedroom, for example, usually contained only a wooden bed with a straw or wool-stuffed mattress, one or two chairs, and a wooden chest. The floor was bare.

Games, Races, and Parades

The Romans loved spectacles. The greatest were the beast shows and gladiatorial fights between men. These were held in an amphitheater—an oval open-air arena packed with sand and surrounded by rows of benches. Government officials sat in front. Then came rich Romans, with ordinary citizens in the rear. People brought picnic baskets with them or purchased sausages, buns, and cold drinks from peddlers on the stairs.

The beast shows took place in the morning. Sometimes the fights were between two animals, such as elephants with iron spikes fastened on their tusks. Sometimes they were between a lion or other big cat and a man armed with a spear. Perhaps a band of archers ran around the arena shooting arrow after arrow into a flock of ostriches or a herd of giraffes. In any event, hundreds of animals might be slaughtered in a single day. Demand ran so high that several species—notably the North African elephant and the Mesopotamian lion—were wiped out.

Gladiatorial fights were held in the afternoon, after business hours. The gladiators were mostly slaves, criminals, and prisoners of war. Occasionally "rich youths or ruined men" became gladiators for a fee. The gladiators trained at special schools located mostly in Rome and Capua. They usually fought with swords,

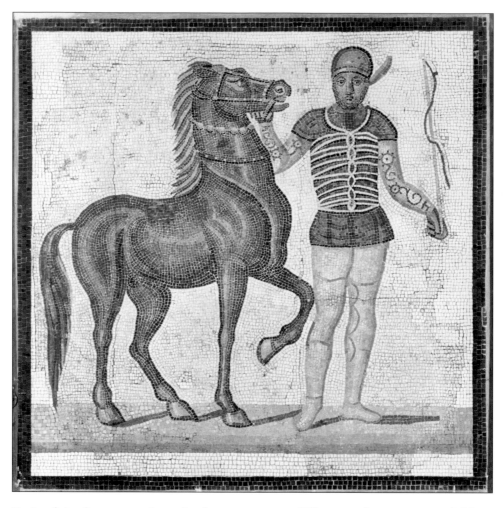

Each of the four teams in a chariot race wore a different color—green, red, blue, or white—to show which racing stable they belonged to. The best racehorses came from Spain and North Africa.

curved daggers, or a net and a trident, a three-pronged spear. Some gladiators used a lasso instead of a net.

The gladiators entered the arena to the sound of blaring trumpets. After parading around, they raised their weapons and greeted the highest-ranking official present with the phrase, "We who are about to die salute you!" Then they fought, usually two at a time.

Only the best survived to win prize money and to fight another day.

Even more popular than gladiatorial combats were the chariot races. These were run for a distance of two and one half to six miles in a stadium called a circus. The chariots had two wheels and were typically drawn by a team of four horses. The drivers were either slaves or members of the lower class. Their main concern was not how fast they could drive but rather how skillfully they could negotiate the turning posts. If they came too close, they risked overturning the chariot. If they went too wide, they lost the inside track and with it, the race. Competition was fierce, and drivers often tried to upset their rivals' chariots. Large sums of money were wagered on the outcome of a race, and a winning driver earned both fame and fortune.

A different kind of spectacle was the triumph, a parade with which the Romans honored a successful general upon his return from battle. Hundreds of thousands of people lined the city's streets, while musicians blew continuously on trumpets and horns. The parade opened with the standards of the victorious legions, together with a statue of the god Jupiter. Next came the spoils of war: baskets filled with coins and jewels, herds of cattle, and especially prisoners and their weapons. These were followed by a gilded chariot carrying the general. He was dressed in purple and gold clothing, with a laurel wreath on his head. Behind him walked senators, magistrates, and other government officials, and behind them marched the victorious legions.

Religious Beliefs and Practices

The Romans were a very religious people. As Cicero explained, "We Romans owe our supremacy over all other peoples to our piety and religious observances and to our wisdom in believing that the spirit of the gods rules and directs everything."

The Romans performed religious observances both privately and publicly. Private observances were led by the paterfamilias of each household. Public observances were led by pontiffs, or priests, who were elected by Roman citizens.

Each Roman household was protected by spirits known as Lares and Penates. The Lares were guardians of the house and farmland. The Penates watched over the storerooms where food was kept. People worshipped their Lares and Penates by burning incense or bits of food before tiny bronze statuettes of the spirits.

The most important public gods were Jupiter, Juno, Minerva, and Mars. Jupiter was god of the sky and father of the Roman state. His symbols included the eagle and the thunderbolt. Juno, Jupiter's wife, was the protector of women and childbirth. Her symbol was the peacock. Minerva was the goddess of wisdom and the protector of craftspeople. She was symbolized by the owl. Mars was the god of war. His symbols were a spear and a shield.

The Romans believed that most of their gods and goddesses

Roman generals always prayed to Mars, the god of war, before they went into battle.

lived in temples, where they were represented by painted marble statues, often adorned with gems and gold. A worshipper would enter a temple, say a prayer with upturned palms, and perhaps burn incense. Sometimes the worshipper would kiss the feet of a statue while whispering requests. "May I be cured of my broken leg." Or "O if only my uncle would pop off!" Worshippers usually left a gift of money or livestock.

Major state sacrifices to the gods were conducted by the pontiffs at an altar in front of a temple. Pontiffs were also responsible for keeping track of the Roman calendar and announcing when festivals would take place. Since these priests were elected and thus sensitive to politics, they sometimes manipulated the calendar. As one historian explained, "They used to stretch out the length of a month to keep a friend in office, or cut short a month to hasten relieving a general of his command." Caesar's reform of the calendar effectively stopped such practices.

The Romans celebrated many religious festivals. The most joyous was undoubtedly the Saturnalia, which was celebrated from

December 17 through December 23. Then schools, law courts, and slave markets were closed. People donned colored costumes and paraded through the streets singing at the top of their lungs. They trimmed their houses with evergreens and exchanged gifts with family members and friends.

The Romans always looked for a sign from the gods before making important military or political decisions. For example, when the Roman army went into battle, a special officer would bring along a coop of sacred chickens. If the chickens gobbled up

In addition to bulls, the animals most commonly used for sacrifices to the gods were sheep, goats, doves, and pigs.

their food before a battle, it meant the Romans would win. If the chickens refused to eat, it meant the Romans would lose. Two other techniques for learning the will of the gods were examining the liver of a sacrificial animal and observing the flight of birds. In the latter case, a priest would mark out a section of the sky as a sacred space. Then he would watch that section to see what kind of bird and how many birds flew through the section and in what direction the birds were going.

Most Romans believed in astrology, which holds that people's lives are influenced by the sun, the moon, the planets, and the signs of the zodiac. Professional astrologers would cast a person's horoscope and advise him or her when to start a new enterprise or go on a journey.

Perhaps because they worshipped so many different gods and goddesses, the Romans were tolerant of religions that came from foreign lands. The two most popular cults centered around Isis and Mithra.

Isis was the Egyptian goddess of marriage and motherhood. Paintings and statues show her with the infant Horus in her arms. She was married to Osiris, who died and, with her help, was reborn. Women were especially devoted to the worship of Isis.

Mithraism, in contrast, was "a man's religion." Women were not admitted to its ceremonies. Mithra was a Persian god of light and truth. Followers of Mithra believed that the world was divided between the forces of good and the forces of evil. It was up to people to help Mithra in his struggle for the good.

PART THREE

The poet Virgil (*center*) was a slow writer. It took him seven years to complete the *Georgics*, which deals mostly with farming, and ten years to write the *Aeneid*, the legendary story of the founding of Rome.

The Ancient Romans
in Their Own Words

Most historians believe Rome was established about 1000 B.C.E. According to legend, however, the city was founded on April 21, 753 B.C.E. by twin brothers named Romulus and Remus. The Roman historian Tacitus (ca. 56–ca. 120 C.E.) recounts part of the legend.

Romulus and Remus conceived a desire to build a city in the area where they had been . . . reared. . . . But these plans were interrupted by their hereditary curse, lust for rule, which resulted in a shameful rivalry. The beginning was innocent enough. Since they were twins and consideration of age could give no priority, they agreed that the guardian gods of the place should choose which should give his name to the new city and rule it when it was built. For awaiting the auguries [signs from the gods] Romulus took the Palatine and Remus the Aventine [two of the seven hills on which Rome was built]. Remus is said to have received the first augury—a flight of six vultures. The omen had already been announced when double the number appeared in Romulus' quarter. Each was hailed king by his own followers, the one party claiming kingship on the basis of priority, the other on the number of the birds. The altercation [quarrel] proceeded from angry taunts to blows, and in the broil Remus was struck down. A commoner story is that in derision [scorn] of his brother, Remus jumped over the new walls, whereupon Romulus slew him in a rage, adding the imprecation [curse]: "Any other who leaps over my walls shall have the same!" Thus Romulus acquired sole power, and the city thus founded was called by its founder's name.

In 215 B.C.E., during one of Rome's wars with the North African city of Carthage, the Roman Assembly passed the Oppian Law. Among other things, it said that women could not wear clothes trimmed with purple except at a religious festival. Twenty years later, after Rome had defeated Carthage, a proposal was made to repeal the Oppian Law. Below is an excerpt from the speech delivered by the conservative senator Marcus Porcius Cato (Cato the Elder) against repeal.

If each man of us, fellow citizens, had established that the right and authority of the husband should be held over the mother of his own family, we should have less difficulty with women in general. . . .

Indeed I blushed when, a short while ago, I walked through the midst of a band of women. Had not respect for the dignity and modesty of certain ones (not them all!) restrained me . . . I should have said, "What kind of behavior is this? Running around in public, blocking streets, and speaking to other women's husbands? Could you not have asked your own husbands the same thing at home? Are you more charming in public with others' husbands than at home with your own? And yet, it is not fitting even at home . . . for you to concern yourselves with what laws are passed or

The women of ancient Rome had few rights under the law and were expected to obey their fathers, husbands, or guardians.

repealed here." Our ancestors did not want women to conduct any—not even private—business without a guardian; they wanted them to be under the authority of parents, brothers, or husbands; we (the gods help us!) even now let them snatch at the government and meddle in the Forum and our assemblies. What are they doing now on the streets and crossroads, if they are not persuading the tribunes to vote for repeal? . . .

If they are victorious now, what will they not attempt? . . . As soon as they begin to be your equals, they will have become your superiors.

The following excerpt is from a speech delivered by the liberal senator Lucius Valerius in favor of repealing the Oppian Law.

While everybody else is to enjoy the recovery of our national prosperity, our wives alone, it seems, are to receive no benefits from the restoration of peace-time conditions. Men, of course, will have purple on their togas if they are magistrates or priests; so will our sons; and so will the big-wigs of the country towns and, here in Rome, even the district officials who, after all, are not the cream of society. To that we shall raise no objection at all—not in their lifetime merely, but even to the extent of their being cremated in their purple when they are dead. But women, if you please, are to be forbidden to wear purple. You, being a man, can have a purple saddle-cloth; the lady who presides over your household will be forbidden to wear a purple cloak; and so your horse will be better turned out than your wife.

In addition to serving in Rome's government, Cato the Elder was an excellent businessman and an active writer. His book *On Agriculture* offered practical advice to anyone interested in buying a farm.

When you are thinking of buying a farm, be sure not to complete the purchase over-hastily, take every trouble to visit it, and do not be satisfied with a single tour of inspection. If it is a good property, the more often you go, the more satisfaction it will give you. Pay attention to how the neighbors' farms look. In a good district they ought to look very well. Be sure not to commit yourself, but go into the farm and inspect it, leaving yourself a way of getting out of the deal. It should have a good climate and be free from storms, and the soil should be naturally fertile. If possible, the foot of the hill is best, facing south in a healthy spot, with a good supply of laborers. The water supply must be plentiful, and it must be near a large town, or the sea or a navigable river, or a good well-used road. You want your farm to be in a district where land does not frequently change hands, and where people regret having sold their property. Be sure that the buildings are in good condition, and do not be over-hasty in rejecting a former owner's advice or methods. A better purchase can be made from a man who is a good farmer and a good builder. When you visit the property, look around to see how many oil-presses and wine-vats there are. If the number is small, then you will know that the harvest is proportionately meager [scanty]. . . . Take care to see that equipment is kept to a minimum to avoid extravagance on the land. Remember that fields are like men; however much profit they make, if they are extravagant, not much is left.

Cato's *On Agriculture* also included the following advice about taking care of sick animals. It is very different from advice that would be given today.

> *If an ox begins to sicken, give him without delay a raw hen's egg and make him swallow it whole. The next day make him drink from a wooden bowl a measure of wine in which has been scraped the head of an onion. Both the ox and his attendant should do these things fasting and standing upright.*
>
> *If a serpent shall bite an ox, or any other quadruped [four-legged animal], take a cup of that extract of fennel which the physicians call smyrnean, and mix it with a measure of old wine. Inject this through his nostrils, and at the same time . . . [cover] the wound with hog's dung. You can treat a man the same way.*
>
> *If a bone is dislocated it can be made sound by this incantation. Take a green reed four or five feet long, cut it in the middle and let two men hold the pieces against your hips. Begin then to chant as follows:*
> "In Alio S.F. Motas Vaeta,
> Daries Dardaries Astataries Dissunapiter."
> *and continue until the free ends of the reed are brought slowly together in front of you. Meanwhile wave a knife above the reeds, and when they come together and one touches the other, seize them in your hand and cut them right and left. These pieces of reed bound upon a dislocated or fractured bone will cure it.*
>
> *But every day repeat the incantation, or in place of it this one:*
> "Huat Hanat Huat
> Ista Pista Sista
> Domiabo Damnaustra."

One of Rome's best-known lyric poets was Gaius Valerius Catullus (ca. 84–ca. 54 B.C.E.). In addition to love poems, he wrote satires in which he poked fun at various individuals, such as "Smiling Egnatius."

Egnatius has teeth that gleam
So shining white, they always seem
To make him smile at any time.
An innocent's accused of crime?
The jury weeps so tearfully?
But he keeps smiling beamingly.
There's mourning at a dead son's bier?
Bereft, a mother sheds a tear?
He's still a-smile. No matter where,
No matter what, his smile's still there.
I think it is a kind of vice
That's neither urbane nor quite nice.
So I must warn you, friend of mine, . . .
To stop your everlasting grin.
For what can be a greater sin
Than smiling when there is no reason,
And grinning in and out of season?

One reason Cicero was a successful lawyer and politician was the fact that he was an eloquent orator. The following is the opening of his first oration against Catiline:

> How much further, Catilina, will you carry your abuse of our forbearance? How much longer will your reckless temper baffle our restraint? What bounds will you set to this display of your uncontrolled audacity? Have you not been impressed by the nightly guards upon the Palatine [one of the seven hills on which Rome was built], by the watching of the city by sentinels? Are you not affected by the alarm of the people, by the rallying of all loyal citizens, by the convening of the senate in this safely-guarded spot, by the looks and expressions of all assembled here? Do you not perceive that your designs are exposed? Do you not see that your conspiracy is even now fully known and detected by all who are here assembled? What you did last night and the night before, where you were and whom you summoned, and what plans you laid, do you suppose that there is one of us here who does not know? Alas! What degenerate days are these! The senate is well aware of the facts, the consul can perceive them; but the criminal still lives. Lives? Yes, lives, and even comes down to the senate, takes part in the public deliberations, and marks down with ominous glances every single one of us for massacre. And we,—such is our bravery,—think we are doing our duty to our country, if we merely keep ourselves out of the way of his reckless words and bloody deeds. No, Catilina, long ere now you should yourself have been led by the consul's orders to execution; and on your own head should have been brought down the destruction which you are now devising for us.

In the past, schoolchildren who studied Latin used to memorize *Gallia est omnis divisa in partes tres.*—"Gaul is a whole divided into three parts." These are the opening words of Caesar's *Commentaries on the Gallic War,* which are written mostly in the third person. The following excerpt describes his invasion of Britain in 55 B.C.E.

The Romans were faced with very grave difficulties. The size of the ships made it impossible to run them aground except in fairly deep water; and the soldiers, unfamiliar with the ground, with their hands full, and weighed down by the heavy burden of their arms, had at the same time to jump down from the ships, get a footing in the waves, and fight the enemy, who, standing on dry land or advancing only a short way into the water, fought with all their limbs unencumbered and on perfectly familiar ground, boldly hurling javelins and galloping their horses, which were trained to this kind of work. These perils frightened our soldiers, who were quite unaccustomed to battles of this kind, with the result that they did not show the same alacrity [briskness] and enthusiasm as they usually did in battles on dry land.

Seeing this, Caesar ordered the warships—which were swifter and easier to handle than the transports, and likely to impress the natives more by their unfamiliar appearance—to be removed a short distance from the others, and then to be rowed hard and run ashore on the enemy's right flank, from which position slings, bows, and artillery could be used by men on deck to drive them back. This maneuver was highly successful. Scared by the strange shape of the warships, the natives halted and then retreated a little. But as the Romans still hesitated, chiefly on account of the depth of the water, the man who carried the eagle of the tenth legion, after praying to the gods that his action might bring good luck to the legion, cried in a loud voice, "Jump down,

Roman warships were called *triremes* because they had three banks of oars. The crocodile on this warship probably means that the ship was based on the Nile River in Egypt.

comrades, unless you want to surrender our eagle to the enemy; I, at any rate, mean to do my duty to my country and my general." With these words he leapt out of the ship and advanced towards the enemy with the eagle in his hands. At this the soldiers, exhorting [urging] each other not to submit to such a disgrace, jumped with one accord from the ship, and the men from the next ships, when they saw them, followed them and advanced against the enemy.

Glossary

aqueduct: A pipe or channel used to transport water from its source to a city water supply; Roman aqueducts were supported by arched bridges when they had to cross gorges and the like.

booty: Goods taken by force, usually from an enemy in time of war.

brazier: A device used for keeping a person warm or grilling food; it consists of a metal pan in which charcoal is burned.

candelabra: A candlestick with several branches.

cavalry: A body of soldiers that fight on horseback.

cult: A religious group centered around the worship of one particular goddess or god.

dictator: An absolute ruler, which the Roman Senate appointed in times of emergency.

dowry: Money, household goods, and property that a bride's family gives her to take into her marriage.

fennel: A sweet-smelling herb.

fungi: Mushrooms and similar organisms.

Ides: Either the thirteenth or the fifteenth day of each month in the Roman calendar; the Ides fell on the fifteenth day in March, May, July, and October.

infantry: A body of soldiers that fight on foot.

javelin: A five-foot-long wooden spear with an iron point.

latrine: A toilet.

legacy: A gift given through a person's will.

mail: A flexible armor formed of overlapping metal rings.

mosaic: A design made by setting small pieces of stone or colored tiles into a surface.

ocher: A pigment made from a mixture of iron ore and clay; its usual colors are yellow, red, or brown.

pedigree: A list of ancestors.

potion: A special drink, usually meant for medical or magical purposes.

tribute: The forced payment of money or property to a conquering or more powerful ruler or nation.

tunic: A loose-fitting, shirtlike garment.

For Further Reading

Bruns, Roger. *Julius Caesar*. New York: Chelsea House, 1987.

Crompton, Samuel Willard. *Julius Caesar*. Philadelphia: Chelsea House, 2003.

Deighton, Hilary J. *A Day in the Life of Ancient Rome*. London: Bristol Classical Press, 1992.

Gunther, John. *Julius Caesar*. New York: Random House, 1959.

Hinds, Kathryn. *The Ancient Romans*. New York: Marshall Cavendish, 2000.

Macdonald, Fiona. *Women in Ancient Rome*. Chicago: NTC/Contemporary, 2000.

Marks, Anthony, and Graham Tingay. *The Romans*. London: Usborne, 1990.

Nardo, Don. *Caesar's Conquest of Gaul*. San Diego: Lucent Books, 1995.

———.*The Importance of Julius Caesar*. San Diego: Lucent Books, 1997.

———.*Life in Ancient Rome*. San Diego: Lucent Books, 1997.

———.*Life of a Roman Soldier*. San Diego: Lucent Books, 2001.

———.*The Roman Republic*. San Diego: Lucent Books, 1994.

Windrow, Martin. *The Roman Legionary*. New York: Franklin Watts, 1984.

ONLINE INFORMATION*

Carr, Karen E. *History for Kids: Ancient Rome*.
   http://www.historyforkids.org/learn/romans/index.htm

Goldberg, Dr. Neil. *The Rome Project*.
   http://www.dalton.org/groups/rome/index.html

McManus, Barbara F. *Rome: Republic to Empire*.
   http://www.vroma.org/~bmcmanus/romanpages.html

Michael C. Carlos Museum of Emory University. *Odyssey Online: Rome*.
   http://carlos.emory.edu/ODYSSEY/ROME/homepg.html

*All Internet sites were available and accurate when this book was sent to press.

Bibliography

Atchity, Kenneth J., ed. *The Classical Roman Reader.* New York: Henry Holt, 1997.

Balsdon, J. P. V. D. *Life and Leisure in Ancient Rome.* New York: McGraw-Hill, 1969.

Bradford, Ernie. *Julius Caesar: The Pursuit of Power.* New York: William Morrow, 1984.

Bruns, Roger. *Julius Caesar.* New York: Chelsea House, 1987.

Carey, John, ed. *Eyewitness to History.* Cambridge: Harvard University Press, 1988.

Casson, Lionel. *Everyday Life in Ancient Rome.* Baltimore: The Johns Hopkins University Press, 1998.

Connolly, Peter, and Hazel Dodge. *The Ancient City.* Oxford: Oxford University Press, 1998.

Cowell, F. R. *Everyday Life in Ancient Rome.* New York: G. P. Putnam's Sons, 1961.

Dupont, Florence. *Daily Life in Ancient Rome.* Oxford: Basil Blackwell, 1992.

Gunther, John. *Julius Caesar.* New York: Random House, 1959.

Hadas, Moses, ed. *The Basic Works of Cicero.* New York: Random House, 1951.

———. *A History of Rome.* Garden City, NY: Doubleday, 1956.

———. *Imperial Rome.* New York: Time, 1963.

Lefkowitz, Mary R., and Maureen B. Fant. *Women's Life in Greece and Rome.* Baltimore: Johns Hopkins University Press, 1982.

Massie, Allan. *The Caesars.* New York: Franklin Watts, 1984.

Nardo, Don. *The Importance of Julius Caesar.* San Diego: Lucent Books, 1997.

———. *Life in Ancient Rome.* San Diego: Lucent Books, 1997.

Tingay, Graham. *Julius Caesar*. Cambridge: Cambridge University Press, 1991.

Wedeck, Harry E., ed. *Classics of Roman Literature*. New York: Philosophical Library, 1963.

Winer, Bart. *Life in the Ancient World*. New York: Random House, 1961.

Workman, B. K. *They Saw It Happen in Classical Times*. Oxford: Basil Blackwell, 1964.

Notes

Part One: The Master of Rome

Page 11 "Keep him": Bradford, *Julius Caesar*, p. 30.
Page 12 "Only twenty talents?": Gunther, *Julius Caesar*, p. 4.
Page 19 "one day's glory": Tingay, *Julius Caesar*, p. 20.
Page 19 "Pompey had the army": Gunther, *Julius Caesar*, p. 70.
Page 22 "strange, white cliffs": Bruns, *Julius Caesar*, p. 69.
Page 27 "The die is cast!": Nardo, *The Importance of Julius Caesar*, p. 50.
Page 27 "raw recruits": Massie, *The Caesars*, p. 31.
Page 33 "Once inside": Bruns, *Julius Caesar*, p. 92.
Page 34 *"Veni, vidi, vici"*: Tingay, *Julius Caesar*, p. 41.
Page 39 "Driven by a mixture": Bruns, *Julius Caesar*, p. 105.
Page 41 "We have killed": Tingay, *Julius Caesar*, p. 107.

Part Two: Everyday Life in the Roman Republic

Page 50 "a good man": Cowell, *Everyday Life in Ancient Rome*, p. 128.
Page 66 "A toga": Cowell, *Everyday Life in Ancient Rome*, p. 75.
Page 71 "rich youths": Winer, *Life in the Ancient World*, p. 196.
Page 74 "We Romans owe": Cowell, *Everyday Life in Ancient Rome*, p. 180.
Page 75 "O if only my uncle": Nardo, *Life in Ancient Rome*, p. 88.
Page 75 "They used to stretch": Winer, *Life in the Ancient World*, pp. 210, 212.
Page 77 "a man's religion": Hadas, *Imperial Rome*, p. 127.

Part Three: The Ancient Romans in Their Own Words

Page 80 "Romulus and Remus": Hadas, *A History of Rome*, pp. 5–6.
Page 81 "If each man of us": Lefkowitz and Fant, *Women's Life in Greece and Rome*, pp. 177–178.
Page 82 "While everybody else": Balsdon, *Life and Leisure in Ancient Rome*, p. 35.
Page 83 "When you are thinking": Workman, *They Saw It Happen in Classical Times*, pp. 78–79.
Page 84 "If an ox begins": Atchity, *The Classical Roman Reader*, pp. 24–25.
Page 85 "Egnatius has teeth": Wedeck, *Classics of Roman Literature*, pp. 12–13.
Page 86 "How much further": Hadas, *The Basic Works of Cicero*, p. 261.
Page 87 "The Romans were faced": Carey, *Eyewitness to History*, pp. 11–12.

Index

Page numbers for illustrations are in **boldface**.

About the Author

"As far back as I can remember, I have been interested in people who came before me—how they lived, what they thought, and what their leaders were like. The desire to know and understand is probably one reason why my favorite reading is mysteries, especially those set in ancient times and different cultures."

In addition to reading mystery novels, Miriam Greenblatt acts in community theater and is an avid adventure traveler. She has rafted rivers in Sumatra and Papua New Guinea, ridden a camel in India and an elephant in Thailand, and explored cities from Tokyo to Timbuktu. She is the author of several history textbooks, three presidential biographies for teenagers, and twelve titles in the Rulers and Their Times series. She lives in a northern suburb of Chicago with her two cats, Batu Khan and Barnum.